The
ABC's
of
Shakespeare

Written by
Kelly Bahney

Illustrated by
Aprilia Muktirina

For Seelie Fae

May you understand Shakespeare, one day

About the Author

Kelly Bahney teaches English Language Arts to high school students in southern Tennessee. She also writes books and independently publishes them under her imprint **Little Owl Publishing**. Little Owlet is a division of Little Owl Publishing that primarily focuses on books for children and other early readers. Sometimes she writes under the name of **Kelly R. Michaels**. To find out more about Kelly or her books, you may visit her website at:

www.kellyrmichaels.com

Copyright © 2018 Kelly Bahney
Little Owlet is a division of **Little Owl Publishing**,
specializing in books for children and young readers

www.kellyrmichaels.com/little-owlet

ISBN: 0989468550
ISBN-13: 978-0-9894685-5-8

Special Thanks

As my first venture into the world of children's literature, this has been my most ambitious project to date, and I certainly hope that it isn't my last. Behind any great project is the invisible support system that helped bring it to life, and so, here I am shedding light upon my wonderful team and donors. Thank you to those that believed in this project enough to fund my crowdsourcing campaign and bring it to life:

Halley
Martha
Kagan
Cay
Jenifer
Jeri
Jeanna

Laura
Beth
Stephanie
Tracie
Kelsa
Alyssa
Jessica

Welcome, welcome! Come one, come all!

Watch the magnificent theater
that is William Shakespeare.

Gather 'round. Read his words, know his ways.
Then you, too, shall understand his plays.

A

is for **Aside**

Aside **An aside is when a character talks to themselves.**
During an **aside**, a character may reveal their thoughts or feelings. The other characters cannot hear the **aside**, but we, the audience, can!

B

is for **Blocking**

Blocking is the movement that actors make.

Walking, dancing, and even eating are all examples of blocking. Blocking may be scripted or even improvised.

C

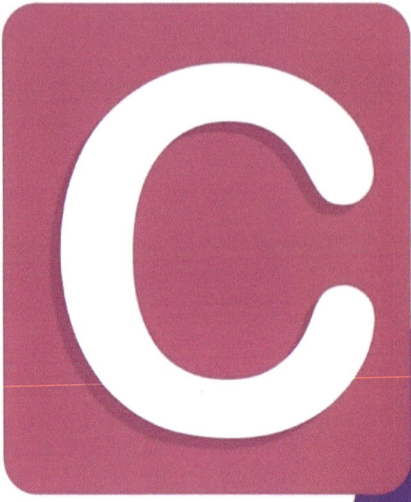

is for Catharsis

Catharsis is when we have strong emotions.

Depending on the play, a **catharsis** can make you laugh or cry. We can all feel a **catharsis** differently.

D is for Dramatis Personae

Dramatis personae means "people of the drama" in Latin.

The **people of the drama** are all the characters we see on stage. They are listed in the beginning of a playscript so we can know how many people are in the play.

E is for Exeunt

Exeunt happens when more than one character leaves the stage.
Exeunt comes from Latin and is where we get the word "exit" from, which is why they look so similar!

F

is for **Foil**

Foil **A foil is a character's opposite**

The **foil** of a hardworking character might be someone who is lazy.

G

is for **Globe Theater**

Globe Theater   The Globe was a theater built by Shakespeare's acting company.

It sat on a certain of the Thames River in the theater district in London.
People would visit the **Globe** to watch Shakespeare's plays, except if it was raining.

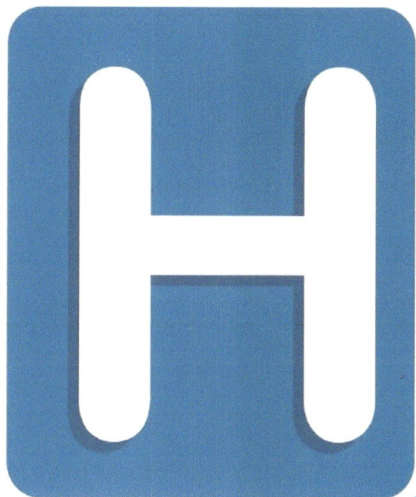

H

is for Hubris

Hubris is bad and is something called a tragic flaw.

Hubris is when a character has a lot of pride. This means that the character thinks very high-ly of themselves, which makes it hard for them to see when they have done something bad.

I is for Irony

"Brutus is an honorable man."

Irony **is when the audience knows things that the characters do not.**
It usually conveys the opposite of what is being said. Shakespeare used three types of **irony**:
dramatic, situational, and verbal.

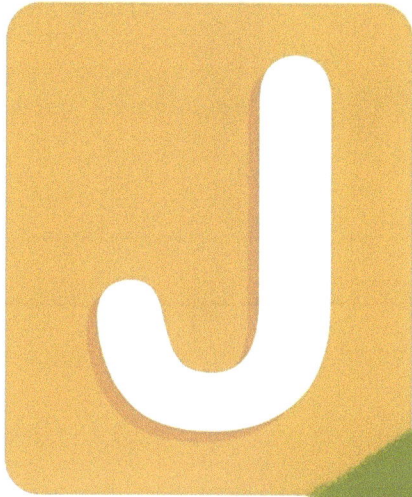

J
is for **Jealousy**

Jealousy is another tragic flaw.

Othello was **jealous** of a man named Iago, and so he thought his wife was cheating on him when she wasn't. Othello also could not see when he had done something bad, and his wife died because of it.

K

is for King

Shakespeare worked for an acting company called The King's Men.

It was named after **King** James I of England took the throne. Shakespeare also wrote about many **kings**, especially English ones.

L

is for **London**

London is England's capital.

Shakespeare spent a lot of time in **London** away from his family to work on his plays. He was a very important figure in the theater world.

M

is for Monologue

Monologue
A monologue is a speech given by a character onstage.

Monologues can last for a long time, but they can only happen when one character speaks. If the **monologue** is directed only to the audience, then it is called a soliloquy.

N

is for **Narrator**

Narrator A narrator gives background information of a story.

A **narrator** speaks to the audience and does not interact with the other characters on stage. The chorus usually plays as Shakespeare's **narrator**.

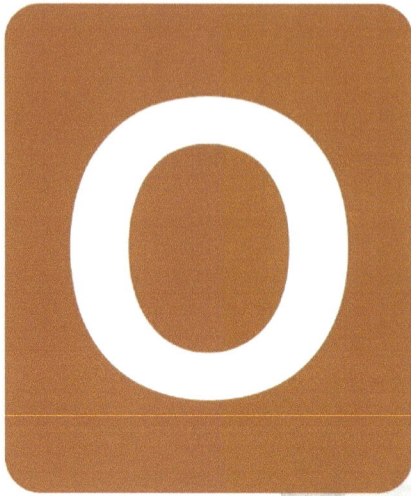

O is for **oxymoron**

PARTING IS SUCH SWEET SORROW

Oxymoron   An oxymoron is a phrase that disagrees with itself.

It may contain several words that mean the opposite of each other.
It is important to pay attention to the oxymoron's context to know what it means.

P

is for PUN

YOU SHALL FIND ME A GRAVE MAN

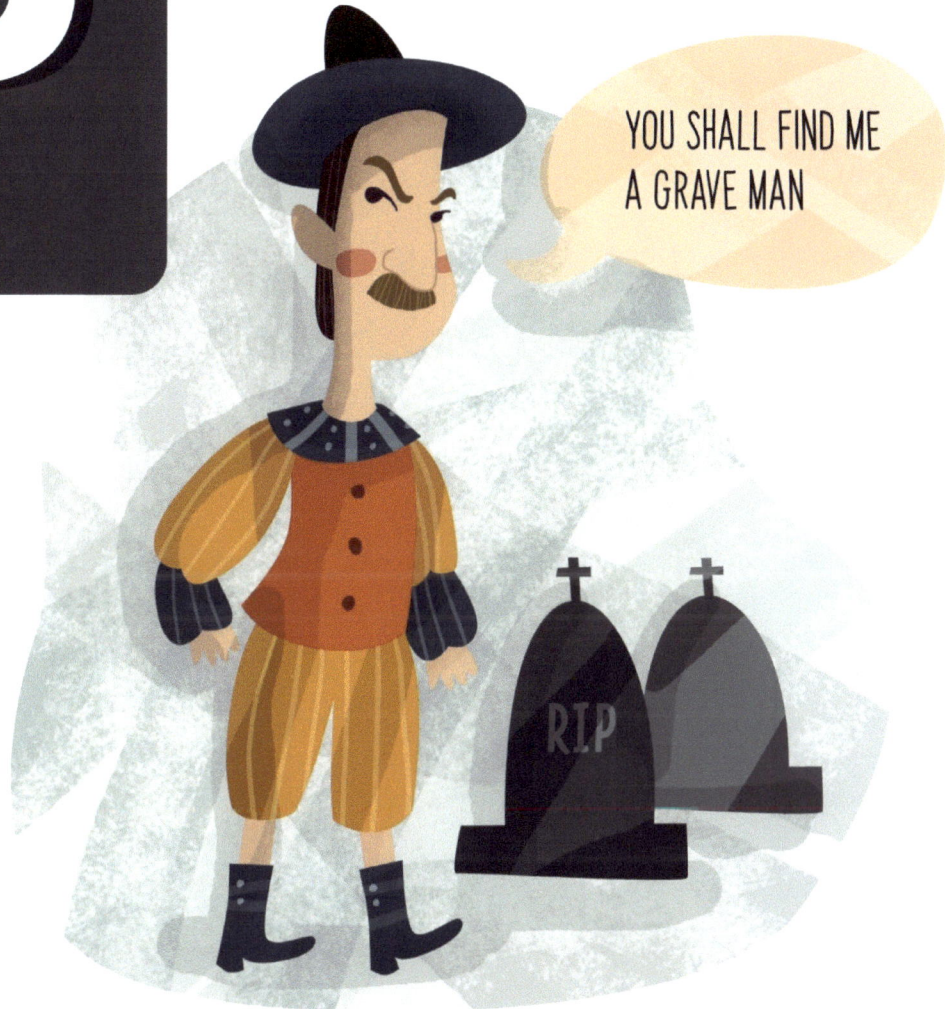

Pun   A pun is like a joke.

It happens when one word can have two different meanings.
We also call this a play on words. Mercutio called himself a grave man.
This meant that he was very serious and that he was about to die.

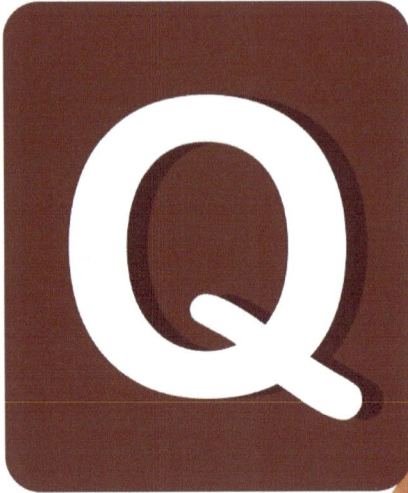

Q

is for **Queen**

Queen

Queen Elizabeth I of England was one of the monarchs during Shakespeare's time.

She was queen for over forty years and never married nor had children during that time.
She did this to show how strong of a leader she could be.
She inspired strong female characters like Portia, Viola, and Beatrice..

R

is for Resolution

Resolution
The resolution is a story's end.

By the **resolution**, all of the problems have been solved and the action is over.

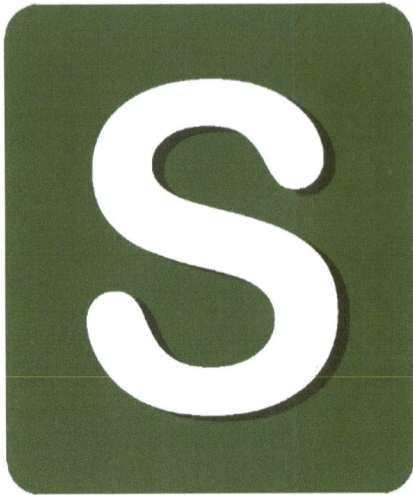

S

is for **Sonnet**

Sonnet **A sonnet is a specific type of poem.**

Sonnets have 14 lines and were usually about love. Every other line rhymes except the last 2, which rhyme with each other. Shakespeare was famous for writing so many **sonnets** that English **sonnets** are also called Shakespearean **sonnets**.

T

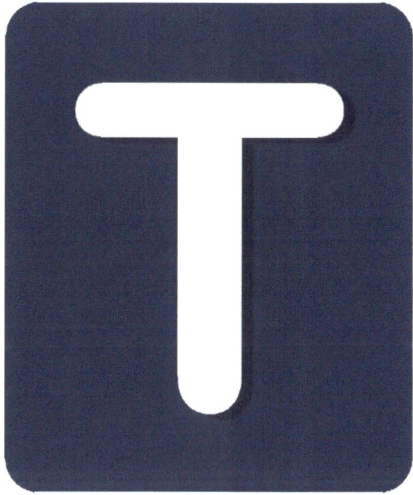

is for **Tragedy**

Tragedy

A tragedy is a type of Shakespeare play that doesn't have a happy ending.

Tragedies have one or more death in them because of a character's tragic flaw, like hubris or jealousy.

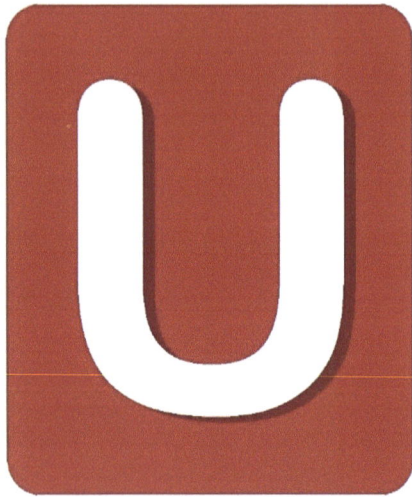

U is for **Understatement**

THIS IS FINE

Understatement

An understatement makes something important seem unimportant.

Understatements can make something interesting or funny, or they can even make people feel better if something bad has happened.

V is for Verse

Sonnet

"My mistress' eyes are nothing like the sun;

Coral is far more red than her lips' red;

If snow be white, why then her breasts are dun;

If hairs be wires, black wires grow on her head."

Verse Verse is the way poems are written.

Poems are divided by lines and stanzas rather than sentences and paragraphs. While poetry is written in **verse**, books are written in a form called "prose," which is how this book is written!

W

is for William Shakespeare

William Shakespeare

William Shakespeare was a writer and actor in the 1500s and 1600s.

He wrote many plays and poems and is the reason we have many words and phrases today. Because of this, many consider **William Shakespeare** to be the "Father of the English Language."

X

is for **Xanthippe**

Xanthippe

Xanthippe is the wife of Socrates, a Greek philosopher.

Xanthippe was never a character in Shakespeare's plays. However, she was mentioned one time to compare her to another woman who was independent as she was. Amazingly, **Xanthippe** is the only word Shakespeare used that began with an "x."

Y is for Yorick

Yorick was a court jester, or clown, in the play HAMLET

Yorick never had a speaking part because he was dead when the play started. Hamlet recognizes his skull when he goes to the graveyard to visit someone else's grave

Z

is for **Zounds!**

ZOUNDS!

Zounds! Zounds is a funny word.

Shakespeare used **zounds** when a character was surprised or angry.
It is a shortened version of "God's wounds!"

Bravo! Applause! Encore!

Our show draws to its close,
And here we offer William's rose—

Our book has ended, but have no doubt.
There is much left to learn, if you just look about.

www.ingramcontent.com/pod-product-compliance
Lightning Source LLC
Chambersburg PA
CBHW042106040426
42448CB00002B/159